Hey Friend!

Thank you for taking the time to read "Do It Yourself DBT for Teens." As a teen therapist, my goal was to create an easy, engaging, and effective tool to aid teenagers as they navigate through their emotions, build and improve relationships, reduce stress, and enhance their overall mental well-being. The unique challenges faced by today's young generation are diverse and complex, and I believe it's fundamental to provide them with the appropriate resources to tackle these issues head-on.

I truly hope that the strategies and insights provided in the book were clear, helpful, and beneficial to either you or your teen. The whole purpose of the workbook is to equip teenagers with the knowledge and tools they need to develop emotional resilience, a skill that is invaluable for their present and future life.

If the book has helped you or your teen in any way, it would mean the world to me to hear about it. Your feedback not only encourages my work but also helps me understand how I can serve you better. If you would like, you can email me at copingskillsforteens@gmail.com

Once again, I appreciate your support and thank you for investing in the emotional health and well-being of your teen. Thanks again!

Warm regards,
Alison Kelly, LPC

Visit Our Websites

To Discover Books, Online Courses, Journals & Workbooks!

WWW.DOITYOURSELFDBT.COM

WWW.COPINGSKILLSFORTEENS.COM

Subscribe To Our Newsletter

Stay updated with NEW products, FREEBIES, and SPECIALS!

Connect With Us

DOITYOURSELFDBT@GMAIL.COM

<u>MENTAL HEALTH DISCLAIMER</u>

These books are not intended to replace professional therapy or medical advice and should be used as a supplement to professional treatment. This workbook is for educational purposes only. Always consult with a qualified healthcare professional before making any changes to your treatment plan.

Radical Acceptance
EMBRACING REALITY

Radical Acceptance
EMBRACING REALITY

LETTING GO OF WHAT YOU CANNOT CONTROL

DO-IT-YOURSELF-DBT
Reality Acceptance Skills (PART 1)

MOVING FORWARD WITH POSITIVITY

REALITY ACCEPTANCE SKILLS 101 - PART 1

Table of Contents

BEING OK WITH THINGS YOU CAN'T CHANGE

RADICALLY ACCEPTING SITUATIONS - PART 2

Table of Contents

BREAKING THE CYCLE OF ANXIETY & STRESS

COPING WITH RADICAL ACCEPTANCE - PART 3

Table of Contents

FOCUSING ON WHAT REALLY MATTERS

RADICAL VALUES AND STRENGTHS - PART 4

Table of Contents

Do you ever get STUCK IN NEGATIVITY?

MOVING FORWARD WITH POSITIVITY

DO-IT-YOURSELF-DBT
Reality Acceptance Skills 101 (PART 1)

Radical Acceptance
WHAT IS IT??

RADICAL ACCEPTANCE is about not fighting reality, and completely accepting something the way it is, so you feel less stressed.

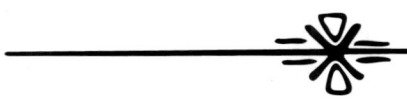

RADICAL ACCEPTANCE is accepting the things you cannot change, and seeing reality for what it is, despite your feelings.

RADICAL ACCEPTANCE is when you accept something, you are releasing judgment and avoiding fighting against it or trying to change it.

When we practice radical acceptance we have a better chance at experiencing life

WHY RADICALLY ACCEPT?

①

Not accepting the reality of a situation is linked to higher rates of emotional distress.

②

Practicing radical acceptance has been shown to reduce feelings of shame, guilt, sadness, and anxiety.

③

Radical acceptance increases happiness, improves relationships, and frees us from frustration.

Radical Acceptance
COPING WITH PAINFUL EMOTIONS

- -

If you're finding it tough to solve a problem or feeling stuck in negative emotions, RADICAL ACCEPTANCE is a powerful tool to alleviate your distress.

RADICAL ACCEPTANCE can help when you find yourself in an unavoidable situation, and accepting the reality can ease your suffering. It's a great way to move forward with a positive attitude and increase happiness!

Accepting Reality
TO ALLEVIATE DISTRESS

Here are five ways to respond when you're feeling stuck and can't seem to find a solution or shift your emotions about a problem:

1. Find solutions to the problem.
2. Change how you feel about the problem.
3. Accept the problem.
4. Keep things as they are and stay stuck.
5. Make things worse by reacting on emotions.

WHICH WAY DO YOU WANT TO RESPOND TO THE PROBLEM?

Accepting Reality
WHY PRACTICE RADICAL ACCEPTANCE

- -

Even though it might seem easier, rejecting reality won't make it magically disappear. It's important for us to acknowledge what's really going on before we can start making positive changes. When we refuse to accept reality, we just end up prolonging our own pain and suffering. By accepting reality, we can move forward and leave negative emotions like unhappiness, anger, shame, sadness, and bitterness behind.

Seeing REALITY for what it is and ACCEPTING the things you CAN'T CHANGE, even if you don't like it.

When we STOP fighting REALITY, things can be GOOD no matter what might be happening in our lives.

A RADICAL EXAMPLE

After going through a breakup, it can be really hard to let go. When we are not able to accept reality as it is; it can keep us holding on to something that is no longer true. Then we suffer unnecessarily because we can't move on from thinking about how things "SHOULD" be instead.

Even if we can accept some parts of the breakup such as our own mistakes, it can be difficult to let go of our thoughts on how things "SHOULD" have been. Accepting the reality of the relationship does not mean that it is still not painful. Accepting "WHAT IS" helps us to move on!

MOVING ON WITH ACCEPTANCE

What are some events, situations, emotions, or people in your life that might need to be radically accepted?

1._____

2._____

3._____

4._____

5._____

6._____

7._____

8._____

9._____

10._____

Ex. I am upset because I did Not get a part in the school play

10 Simple Steps To
RADICAL ACCEPTANCE

- -

1) ACKNOWLEDGE: Acknowledge the situation without passing judgment; facts are facts, even if they are unwanted - "This is how it is, and I can't change it."

2) NOTICE: Notice if you find yourself resisting the reality with thoughts like, "This is not how it should be."

3) FACTS: Keep in mind the facts of the current situation and that it cannot be changed at the moment - "It is what it is."

4) ALLOW: Allow yourself to feel disappointment, anger, sadness, or grief - "I feel so uncomfortable with things."

5) RECOGNIZE: Recognize that the situation may be causing you to feel overwhelmed, and you might feel more relieved if you could let it go - "I would feel better if I stopped focusing on what is wrong."

6) SUPPORT: Support yourself by planning to accept the situation by using positive self-talk, relaxation techniques, and mindfulness - "When I have a confident mindset, it helps me stay calm."

7) IMAGINE: Imagine accepting what seems unacceptable and all the things you could do if you did accept the facts - "I would feel less stressed and able to enjoy work if I accepted things."

8) REALIZE: Realize that life can still be joyous even with painful events and discomfort in it - "I don't like feeling this way, but I can still enjoy the moment by not resisting what is."

9) ACCEPTANCE: Accept the situation completely and stop fighting reality. - "I cannot do anything about what happened, and that is okay."

10) PRACTICE: Practice radically accepting, and know that it make take some time to get used to - "Even though negative thoughts and feeling might come back around, I will keep working on accepting the situation until I feel better."

What would you like
TO MOVE ON FROM?

- -

WHAT CURRENT SITUATION DO YOU FEEL STUCK IN?

_____

_____

_____

I am upset because I did Not get a part in the school play

1) ACKNOWLEDGE: What are the facts of the situation?

_____

_____

30 people auditioned for the play and only 15 got parts

2) NOTICE: How are you questioning or fighting reality?

_____

_____

I think I had a good audition...even better than most

3) FACTS: What is the reality of the situation that cannot be changed right now?

_____

_____

I did not get offered a part in the school play this year

4) ALLOW: How can you allow yourself to feel your emotions?

_____

_____

By not letting my disappointment get in the way

5) RECOGNIZE: What feelings come up when you think about accepting the reality of the situation?

_____

_____

More calm and excited to try something new instead

6) SUPPORT: How can you accept reality?

_____

_____

Know I did my best & look forward to auditioning again

7) IMAGINE: What would you do if you accepted the facts?

_____

_____

_____

I can focus on doing more fun things like horseback riding

8) REALIZE: How can your life still be joyous even with painful events and discomfort in it?

_____

_____

_____

I can be happy for & support my friends in the play

9) ACCEPTANCE: How can you stop fighting reality and radically accept the situation completely and totally?

_____

_____

_____

Tell myself that "it's a bummer but I will be okay"

10) PRACTICE: How can you practice what you can do or what you can say to yourself while accepting reality?

_____

_____

_____

_____

_____

To journal my feelings & Radical acceptance statements

Keep Repeating "I don't like it but I can accept it"

RADICAL ACCEPTANCE CHEAT SHEET

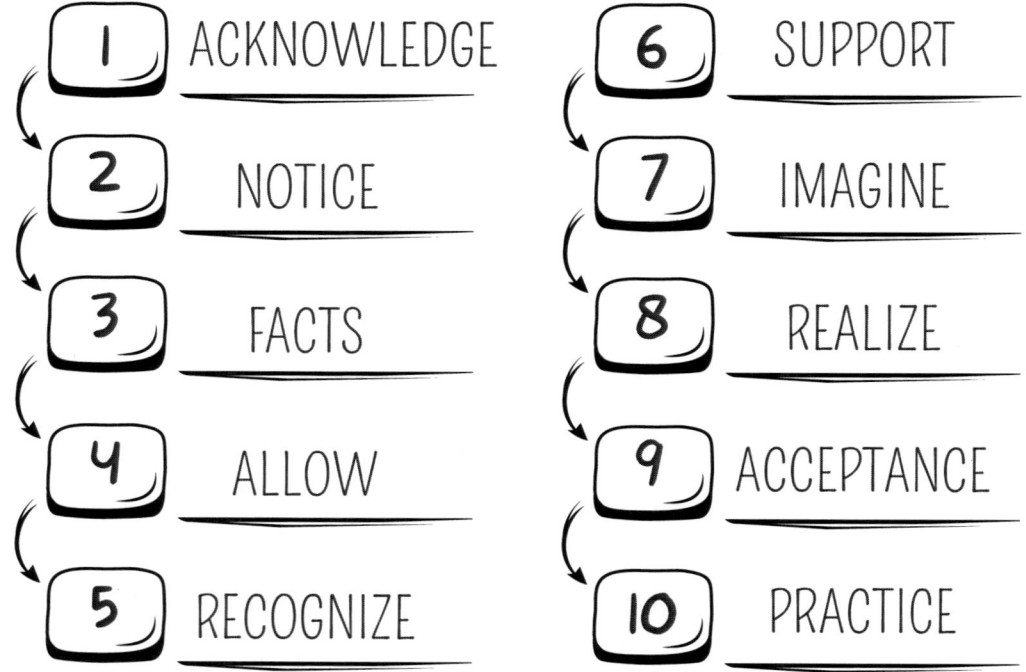

1 ACKNOWLEDGE
2 NOTICE
3 FACTS
4 ALLOW
5 RECOGNIZE

6 SUPPORT
7 IMAGINE
8 REALIZE
9 ACCEPTANCE
10 PRACTICE

FACTORS THAT INTERFERE WITH ACCEPTANCE

1. You believe that it is too difficult or you are incapable of accepting really painful events and facts.

2. You think by accepting an unwanted situation, you are "giving up" or will be unable to change or prevent any future upsets.

3. Your emotions such as anger, sadness, or shame get in the way of being able to accept the situation.

WHEN YOU ARE NOT IN ACCEPTANCE

- Telling yourself it would be okay if only X would happen
- Thinking it shouldn't be this way
- Saying this doesn't make any sense
- Feeling resentment, bitter, shame, guilt, or anger
- Trying to control other people's behavior
- Refusing to accept things
- Trying to predict the future
- Giving up
- Feeling victimized or beaten down
- Thinking you shouldn't feel like this
- Making judgments or criticisms
- Only accepting certain parts of the situation

RADICAL ACCEPTANCE ROADBLOCKS

- That you are 100% okay with the situation
- Denying how you feel or how the situation affects you
- Giving up on things or wanted change
- That you approve of the situation or found it "acceptable"
- Excusing unhealthy behaviors
- Letting people off the hook for being hurtful
- Not acknowledging the stress of the situation

RADICAL ACCEPTANCE REALIZATIONS

- Rejecting reality doesn't change it
- Changing reality requires accepting it
- Pain is unavoidable
- Rejecting reality turns pain into suffering
- Refusing to accept reality keeps you stuck in unhappiness, bitterness, anger, sadness, and shame
- Acceptance may lead to sadness, but calmness usually follows

What am I willing to
ACCEPT RIGHT NOW?

1) Three things I can
accept today:

☐ ....
☐ ....
☐ ....

2) Three small things I
can accept right now:

☐ ....
☐ ....
☐ ....

3) Three big things I
can accept right now:

☐ ....
☐ ....
☐ ....

4) Three things from the
past I can accept right now:

☐ ....
☐ ....
☐ ....

NOT PRACTICING ACCEPTANCE

When faced with difficult situations, the idea of "just accepting it" can be incredibly challenging. It can feel impossible to accept something that seems unacceptable. The idea of accepting reality may also seem like giving up on the possibility of change. However, acceptance does not diminish what you are going through or that you are okay with it. Instead, by refraining from resisting what is actually happening, we can still feel distress but avoid unnecessary suffering.

PRACTICE RADICAL ACCEPTANCE

Practicing RADICAL ACCEPTANCE everyday with small things will help to create a habit. Practice when in traffic or waiting in a long line. Practice it when a someone is rude towards you. Practice when you are feeling nervous or annoyed. By practicing RADICAL ACCEPTANCE in less emotionally intense situations, your mind will create new pathways.

Radical Acceptance
COPING AFFIRMATIONS

- I can handle what is in front of me as it is.
- Life is worth living, even if I am in pain.
- Life has ups and downs. Downs are inevitable.
- Fighting the past only blinds me from the present.
- I can live in the present, despite the pain I am experiencing.
- I can have pain without it turning into suffering.
- I can handle it, even if I am unhappy with what is happening.
- I can't change what has already happened.
- I can learn from the past to solve my present problems.
- My past does not define my future.
- How I react in this moment is all I have control over.
- I see the present moment for what it is.
- I can't change the situation, but I can control how I respond to it.
- I don't understand why this is happening, but I can accept it.
- This is how it has to be. I can't change the past.

Radical Acceptance
COPING AFFIRMATIONS

- -

- I am strong, I will survive the present crisis.

- I can't go back in time. I can't control the past.

- I will not always agree or like it. That's ok.

- This situation won't last forever.

- I've already been through other painful experiences and been okay.

- My feelings are uncomfortable right now, but I can accept them.

- I can be anxious and still deal with the situation.

- I'm strong enough to handle what's happening to me right now.

- This is an opportunity to learn how to cope with my fears.

- I can ride this out and not let it get to me.

- I can take all the time I need right now to let go and relax.

- These are just my feelings, and eventually they'll go away.

- I'm strong and I can deal with this.

Radical Acceptance
COPING AFFIRMATIONS

- I've survived other situations like this before, and I'll survive this one too.

- My anxiety/fear/sadness won't kill me; it just doesn't feel good right now.

- It's okay to feel sad/anxious/afraid sometimes.

- My thoughts don't control my life, I do.

- I can think different thoughts if I want to.

- I'm not in danger right now.

- This situation stinks, but it's only temporary.

- This too shall pass.

RADICAL COPING

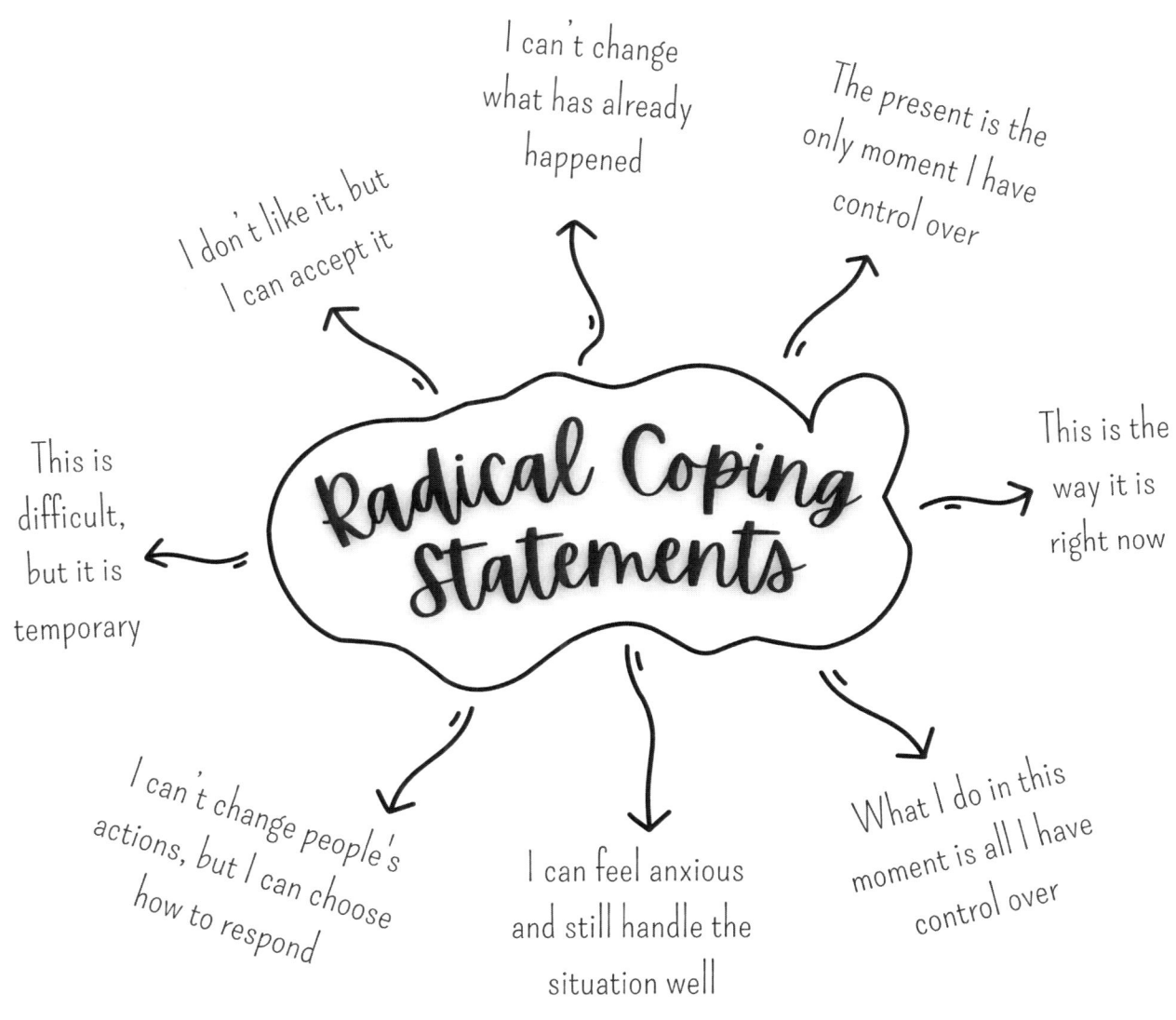

I can't change
what has already
happened

The present is the
only moment I have
control over

I don't like it, but
I can accept it

This is the
way it is
right now

This is
difficult,
but it is
temporary

Radical Coping Statements

I can't change people's
actions, but I can choose
how to respond

I can feel anxious
and still handle the
situation well

What I do in this
moment is all I have
control over

MY FAVORITE COPING STATEMENTS:

_____

_____

_____

_____

How do you accept
THINGS AS THEY ARE?

BEING OK WITH THINGS YOU CAN'T CHANGE

DO-IT-YOURSELF-DBT
Radically Accepting Situations (PART 2)

Radical Acceptance
FOR CHANGE

- -

① RADICAL ACCEPTANCE is about accepting the things you can't change.

② RADICAL ACCEPTANCE can reduce distress and increase feelings of freedom.

③ RADICAL ACCEPTANCE is when we are able to accept life just as it is, even if we don't like it.

WHEN IS ACCEPTANCE NEEDED?

- -

- When stressful events happen in your life and you cannot fix them, change them, or make them go away.

- When you are you stuck in unhappiness, anger, shame, sadness, or other painful emotions from refusing to accept reality.

- When it's hard to accept things you don't like or that cause distress.

- When you want to work through difficulty but find it challenging.

PRACTICE RADICAL ACCEPTANCE

Have you ever struggled with wanting to change
something in your life that is difficult to accept?
Do you find yourself worrying about the future?
Are there things in you regret or wish did not happen?

There are so many things we don't have control over. We
can't change the past and we can't know the future. But,
we can have the willingness to tolerate something as it is
in the moment, while working to change it!

What are you willing to ACCEPT AND CHANGE?

I radically accept [   ], and I will work to change [   ].

Example:

- I radically accept my grades, and I will work to change my study habits.

- I radically accept not having as many friends as I would like, and I will work to expand my social circle.

- I radically accept wanting to get into my dream college, and I will look into other schools that may also be a good fit for me.

- I radically accept that my leg has to be in a cast for 2 more weeks, and I will find solutions to work around it.

ACCEPTANCE AND CHANGE

I radically accept _____

And I will work to:

- [ ] Explore
- [ ] Identify
- [ ] Move
- [ ] Help
- [ ] Apply

- [ ] Discover
- [ ] Find
- [ ] Reduce
- [ ] Make
- [ ] Close
- [ ] Follow-up

- [ ] Add
- [ ] Change
- [ ] Not
- [ ] Think
- [ ] Ask
- [ ] Switch

_____

_____

- -

I radically accept _____

And I will work to:

- [ ] Explore
- [ ] Identify
- [ ] Move
- [ ] Help
- [ ] Apply

- [ ] Discover
- [ ] Find
- [ ] Reduce
- [ ] Make
- [ ] Close
- [ ] Follow-up

- [ ] Add
- [ ] Change
- [ ] Not
- [ ] Think
- [ ] Ask
- [ ] Switch

_____

_____

ACCEPTANCE AND CHANGE

- -

I radically accept _____

And I will work to:

☐ Explore   ☐ Discover   ☐ Add

☐ Identify   ☐ Find   ☐ Change

☐ Move   ☐ Reduce   ☐ Not

☐ Help   ☐ Make   ☐ Think

☐ Apply   ☐ Close   ☐ Ask

     ☐ Follow-up   ☐ Switch

_____

_____

- -

I radically accept _____

And I will work to:

☐ Explore   ☐ Discover   ☐ Add

☐ Identify   ☐ Find   ☐ Change

☐ Move   ☐ Reduce   ☐ Not

☐ Help   ☐ Make   ☐ Think

☐ Apply   ☐ Close   ☐ Ask

     ☐ Follow-up   ☐ Switch

_____

_____

7 Steps To Working Through RADICAL ACCEPTANCE

1) Write down 2 situations that you wish were different or not the outcome you wanted, to practice RADICAL ACCEPTANCE:

A. _____

Example: "Some people got to exempt presenting to the class and others did not"

B. _____

Example: "My friend has a big personality and embarrasses me in social situations"

2) What is getting in the way of not being able to RADICALLY ACCEPT these situations:

A. _____

Example: "Accepting my teachers decision on who could exempt presenting"

B. _____

Example: "I wish my friend would act differently around others"

It's okay if you don't know...keep working it through and see if you can shift your thoughts and feelings to accept the situation!

RADICALLY ACCEPT THE SITUATION

3) Notice where you are resisting reality:

Example: A: "This shouldn't be happening" or B: "They need to be different"

4) Keep in mind that some things cannot be changed:

Example: A: "It is out of my control" or B: "It is just who they are"

5) Identify what has led up to this moment:

Example: A: "It is happening because..." or B: "They are acting that way because..."

PROS AND CONS

6) What would your choice be if you <u>DO</u> accept the situation?

A. _____

Example: "Some people got to exempt presenting to the class and others did not"

PROS	CONS
Example: Have more peace & calm	Example: Fearful it might happen again

B. _____

Example: "My friend has a big personality and embarrasses me in social situations"

PROS	CONS
Example: Enjoy my time with them	Example: The friendship might end

PROS AND CONS

7) What would your choice be if you <u>DON'T</u> accept the situation?

A. _____

Example: "Some people got to exempt presenting to the class and others did not"

PROS	CONS
Example: Fight for fairness	Example: Feeling angry and dislike the class

B. _____

Example: "My friend has a big personality and embarrasses me in social situations"

PROS	CONS
Example: Help my friend change their behavior	Example: Not wanting to include my friend

RADICAL ACCEPTANCE OF OTHERS

1) What is the name of the person who is causing you distress?

Example: Jill (a friend from school)

2) What is (name of person) doing to cause you pain?

Example: She is ignoring me during class and only wants to talk to me at night when she is bored

3) What would I like (name of person) to do instead?

Example: I would like her to act like my friend during school by including me in her conversations

4) How have I tried to get (name of person) to (do what I need)?

Example: I have asked her why she ignores me in class and asked her to include me more

5) Even though I have (done these things) to try and get (name of person) to (do what I need) they still continue to (do what I dislike) which makes me feel:

- [ ] Hopeless
- [ ] Anxious
- [ ] Nervous
- [ ] Vunerable
- [ ] Angry
- [ ] Fearful
- [ ] Guilty

- [ ] Ashamed
- [ ] Stressed
- [ ] Panicked
- [ ] Teary
- [ ] Empty
- [ ] Guarded
- [ ] Resentful

- [ ] Lonley
- [ ] Sad
- [ ] Indifferent
- [ ] Annoyed
- [ ] Self-conscious
- [ ] Insecure
- [ ] Disappointed

6) In order to experience freedom from feeling (what I feel), I am willing to accept that (name of person) actions are out of my control and I can only control my own thoughts, feelings, and behaviors.

- [ ] Yes
- [ ] No
- [ ] Maybe

7) If no or maybe, what part of the situation could you accept? _____
_____
_____

Example: I could accept that the friendship is not as valued by her as much as it is to me

8) Is there a boundary needed or a compromise you could make? _____
_____
_____

Example: I could stop investing so much time into the friendship such as not talking to her as much

PUTTING IT ALL TOGETHER

- -

9) NOW TRY THIS: Even though, I do not approve of or feel happy about (name of person) choices, I am willing to accept (name of person) exactly as they are. In doing so, I am able to focus on what makes me happy, take care of myself, and establish any necessary boundaries for my own wellbeing.

HOW DO YOU FEEL NOW THAT YOU HAVE RADICALLY ACCEPTED THE SITUATION?

☐ Happier	☐ Excited	☐ Proud
☐ Calmer	☐ Pleased	☐ Carefree
☐ Peaceful	☐ Relaxed	☐ Relieved
☐ Grounded	☐ Enthusiastic	☐ Positive
☐ Content	☐ Determined	☐ Trusting
☐ Optimistic	☐ Inspired	☐ Comfortable
☐ Confident	☐ Strong	☐ Curious

Other thoughts and feelings: _____

_____

_____

Radical Acceptance
FOR STRESSFUL SITUATIONS

Reflect on past stressful situations to help you radically accept the reality of a current experience and view it in a different way.

1) What is stressful about this situation?

Example: I really wanted to make the lacrosse team and thought I did well at try-outs, but did not make the team.

2) What events have led up to this situation?

Example: My sibling made the lacrosse team when they were in high school and it seemed like fun.

3) How have you contributed to the development of this situation?

Example: I decided not to try out for any other sports because I assumed I would make the lacrosse team since my sibling was on it.

4) How have others contributed to the development of this situation?

Example: My parents encouraged me to focus on lacrosse even though I wanted to try golf too.

5) What in this situation do you have control over?

Example: I can talk to coach and see what skills I am lacking, Then I can practice more and try-out for next season.

6) What in this situation do you NOT have control over?

Example: I can't make or convince coach to let me on the team.

7) How did you respond/react to this situation?

Example: I was mad. I thought the coach was being unfair and showing favorites. I took my frustrations out on my parents and skipped school the next day.

8) How did your response/reaction make you feel?

Example: I felt guilty for yelling at my parents when they were just trying to listen and be supportive. I also regretted missing school because I got behind in my schoolwork and was grounded from seeing my friends for the weekend. It just made things worse.

9) How did your response/reaction make others feel?

Example: My parents were disappointed with my reaction.

10) How could you have responded differently to this situation?

Example: I could have been more calm and talked to my parents about my frustration. I could have done something fun to distract myself like hanging out with a friend.

11) If you had radically accepted this situation instead of reacting, how would the outcome be different?

Example: Accepting that I did not make the team would have made me less reactive and I would have been able to think through things more clearly. I probably would have gotten over my frustration much faster.

UNWANTED REALITY

WAYS TO ACCEPT REALITY

Radical Acceptance
IN THE MOMENT

By focusing on the current moment without judgment, it allows us to radically accept the facts of the current situation as it is.

UNWANTED REALITY

Example: I am failing my history class and grounded until I bring my grade up, which makes me feel anxious

WAYS TO ACCEPT REALITY

Example: I am failing history because I have not been studying for my tests. If I start studying for tests ahead of time, I will do better. I can also ask my teacher for recovery or extra credit to raise my grade.

Accepting In The Moment
WHAT YOU CAN & CAN'T CONTROL

Do you ever find yourself wanting to have control over everything in your life? It's completely understandable, but it can be challenging to accept that we can't control everything. Although we may not have control over the world around us, we do have the ability to control our reactions to it.

By learning to accept and deal with situations that are out of our control, we can find inner peace and tranquility. This can also be beneficial in reducing stress and anxiety.

Some things you CAN CONTROL

- How you talk to yourself
- The way you treat other people
- The people you spend time with
- Practicing personal growth
- Your mindset
- Where you put your energy
- Your favorite tv shows
- Letting go of grudges

- How you practice self-care
- The music you listen to
- How kind you are to others
- What you are grateful for
- How you spend your time
- What you wear
- The art you create
- What music you listen to

Some things you
CANNOT CONTROL

- What other people do
- How other people see you
- How other people treat you
- Life not being fair
- What other people think or feel
- Being left out
- The future
- Natural disasters
- Who your family is

- Certain outcomes
- The past
- That change is inevitable
- If people like or dislike you
- The weather
- Someone else's choices
- The passing of time
- Physical and mental limitations
- Others reactivity in situations

How do you
AVOID DISCOMFORT?

BREAKING THE CYCLE
OF ANXIETY & STRESS

DO-IT-YOURSELF-DBT
Coping With Radical Acceptance (PART 3)

COPING WITH NON-ACCEPTANCE

It's normal for people to avoid discomfort by coping in unhealthy ways, such as ignoring, resisting, or rejecting the situation. While this may temporarily minimize the discomfort, it can cause an increase in distress and misery.

Radical acceptance is all about how we handle those tough situations. Instead of reacting in a negative or impulsive way, we choose to embrace reality and break free from those unhappy, angry, or guilty feelings. It's all about accepting the situation and making a real change for the better, especially when it's causing us distress.

Common ways people
RESPOND TO DISCOMFORT

- -

1) <u>Problem Solving</u> – Acknowledging the reality of the situation. Then changing what you can, and accepting what you cannot control.

2) <u>Changing The Outlook</u> - Finding meaning or value in the situation. Then looking at it from a more positive perspective to build acceptance.

3) <u>Turning the Mind</u> – Learning to tolerate the reality of the situation, even if you don't agree with it, and responding in a more confident way.

4) <u>Staying Miserable</u> – Resisting the reality of the situation, which will only worsen an already distressful and unhappy experience.

1) PROBLEM SOLVING

Acknowledging the reality of the situation. Then changing what you can, and accepting what you cannot control.

1) PROBLEM SOLVING –

How can you acknowledge the reality of the situation?

_____

_____

What about the situation can you accept that you can't you control?

_____

_____

2) CHANGING THE OUTLOOK

Finding meaning or value in the situation. Then looking at it from a more positive perspective to build acceptance.

2) CHANGING THE OUTLOOK -

How can you find meaning or value in the situation?

_ _

_ _

What is a way you can look at the situation from a different perspective?

_ _

_ _

3) TURNING THE MIND

Learning to tolerate the reality of the situation, even if you don't agree with it, and responding in a more confident way.

3) TURNING THE MIND –

How can you learn to tolerate the reality of the situation?

_____

_____

How can you respond in a more confident way?

_____

_____

4) STAYING MISERABLE

Resisting the reality of the situation, which will only worsen an already distressful and unhappy experience.

4) STAYING MISERABLE –

Are you resisting the reality of the situation?

_ _

_ _

How is not accepting the reality of the situation causing you distress?

_ _

_ _

Blocks To Coping
BY BEING WILLING OR UNWILLING

- -

We all face our fair share of tough times: dealing with different situations, experiences, and emotions. Our goal is to make things easier, bring about change, or just get through these situations. The funny thing is, sometimes we unintentionally end up making our experiences even more difficult.

Being willing means understanding what a situation needs in order to be successful and responding accordingly. On the flip side, unwillingness occurs when we only consider our own desires and insist on being right.

WILLING

Being WILLING is BEING OPEN and doing what is RIGHT in the moment by acting with AWARENESS from your WISE MIND.

- WILLING TO be flexible and not fighting against reality

- WILLING TO do what is most effective in each situation

- WILLING TO act from your highest self and your deepest core values

- WILLING TO listen to the person you are interacting with

- WILLING TO ask yourself if the situation would cause distress in five years

WHEN ARE YOU WILLING?

When is a time when you were willing to work toward a resolution?

_____

_____

_____

What was your anticipated outcome of being willing to try?

_____

_____

_____

What was the benefit to you of choosing to be willing?

_____

_____

_____

How did you find being willing difficult?

_____

_____

_____

How would being unwilling in this situation have created more distress?

_____

_____

_____

UNWILLING

Being UNWILLING to TOLERATE the moment and REFUSING to make the CHANGES that are NEEDED

- UNWILLING TO let go of control or not being proven wrong

- UNWILLING TO work with others or be flexible

- UNWILLING TO make changes that are needed

- UNWILLING TO listen to suggestions that will improve the situation

- UNWILLING TO change something that can be changed

WHEN ARE YOU UNWILLING?

When is a time when you were unwilling to work toward a resolution?

_____

_____

_____

What was your anticipated outcome of being unwilling to try?

_____

_____

_____

What was the cost of choosing to be unwilling?

_____

_____

_____

How did you find being unwilling difficult?

_____

_____

_____

How would being willing in this situation have helped to make it better?

_____

_____

_____

How to change
UNWILLING TO WILLING
STEP-BY-STEP

① Notice when you are being UNWILLING in a situation.
- "What can't I accept?"
- "What am I resisting?"
- "How am I being closed-minded?"

② What are your THOUGHTS about the situation?
- "How does it affect me or others?"
- "What do I have to do with it?"
- "Why am I being resistant?"

③ What are your FEELINGS about the situation?
- "Do I feel angry, irritated, anxious, sad, or something else?"

④ What are your REACTION urges to the situation?
- "Do I want to walk away, fight back, create conflict, avoid conflict, or something else?"

⑤ Can you RADICALLY ACCEPT the situation as it is?

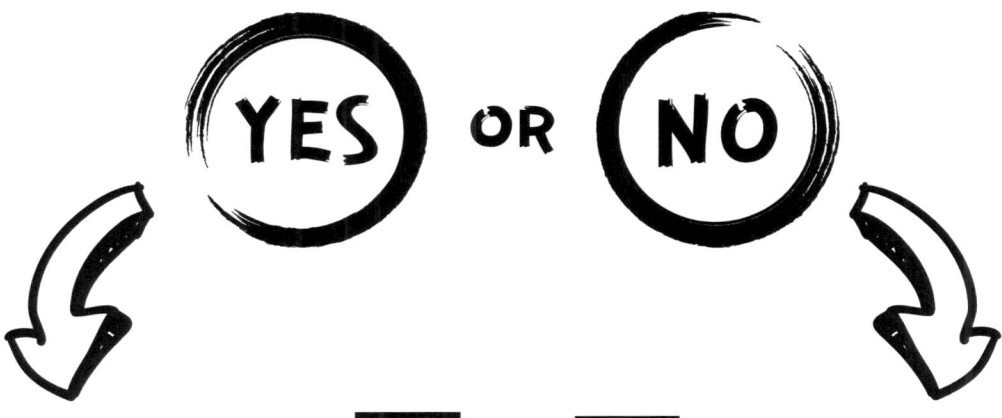

YES OR NO

YES →

1) ALLOWING the situation to be just what it is

2) Listening to your WISE MIND and deciding what to do

3) PARTICIPATING fully and doing what is needed to be effective

NO →

1) NON-JUDGMENTALLY accept your unwillingness

2) TURN YOUR MIND toward acceptance and willingness

3) Try OPEN HANDS, HALF-SMILING, and a WILLING POSTURE

⑥ If you still unable to change or challenge your UNWILLINGNESS to WILLINGNESS, then ask yourself ... "What am I afraid of?" "What is in the way of being willing?"

How to change
UNWILLING TO WILLING

STEP-BY-STEP

(1) Notice when you are being UNWILLING in a situation:

_____

_____

(2) What are your THOUGHTS about the situation?

_____

_____

(3) What are your FEELINGS about the situation?

_____

_____

(4) What are your REACTION urges to the situation?

_____

_____

(5) Can you RADICALLY ACCEPT the situation as it is?

_____

_____

(6) If you still unable to change or challenge your UNWILLINGNESS to WILLINGNESS, then ask yourself ...What am I afraid of?" "What is in the way of being willing?"

_____

_____

UNWILLINGNESS VS. ACCEPTANCE

It shouldn't be this way  I did not want it to be like this, but it's reality

It's not fair  This is uncomfortable, but I can handle it

They should know better  Maybe they did not understand what I wanted

I am always overacting to my feelings  I can't always control my emotions, but they matter

Why do bad things keep happing to me?  Sometimes random things happen that we don't like

I shouldn't have to tell them over-and-over  I need to tell them how I feel, so they understand

UNWILLINGNESS VS. ACCEPTANCE

TURNING THE MIND

REJECTION 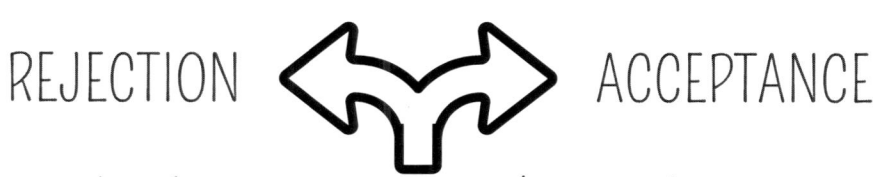 ACCEPTANCE

When presented with a situation we can't control, we can either choose REJECTION or ACCEPTANCE. Rejecting reality by trying to escape what is, blocking things out, or hiding emotions; can cause us to feel more distressed and resentful. If we can TURN THE MIND toward ACCEPTANCE, it puts us in the direction of calmness and joy.

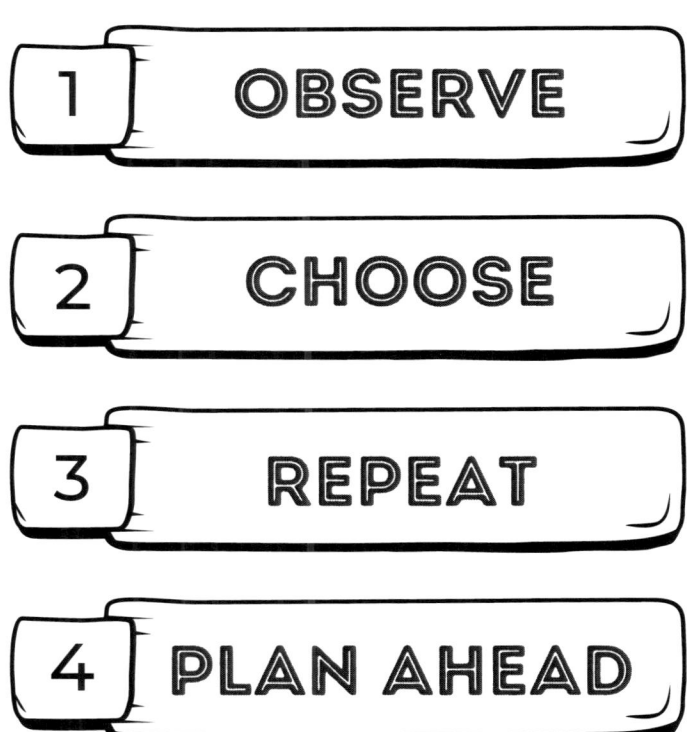

1 OBSERVE

2 CHOOSE

3 REPEAT

4 PLAN AHEAD

TURNING THE MIND

1) OBSERVE when you are not accepting reality:
- What are you feeling?...angry, sad, anxious, jealous, frustrated, hurt

Example: "Angry and annoyed"

- What are you thinking?...why me? it's not fair! this shouldn't be happening!

Example: "I can't handle this! It makes me feel so upset that things never change!"

2) CHOOSE to accept reality as it is.
- Imagine what acceptance might look like:

Example: "Attending school even if I don't want to go"

- Imagine what acceptance might feel like:

Example: "Good because my grades have gone up"

TURNING THE MIND

3) REPEAT steps 1 & 2 every time you notice your mind moving back toward rejection and away from acceptance.

>
>
>
>
> Example: "When I get upset, I can take a breath and turn my mind back to acceptance"

4) PLAN AHEAD and develop a strategy to cope with future situations that may be hard to accept reality.

>
>
>
>
> Example: "Next time my plans are cancelled, I will stay calm and figure out what to do next"

Accepting Reality
WITH YOUR BODY

HALF-SMILING

We all go through tough times when it feels like it's almost impossible to put on a smile. The HALF-SMILE technique can be used to find some peace and calm amidst the chaos. By using the HALF-SMILE technique, you can relax your body and mind, and maybe even accept the reality of the situation a little easier.

HOW TO HALF-SMILE

<u>1st</u> - Relax the muscles in your face, from the top of your head to your chin. You can also try tensing your facial muscles and then relaxing them.

<u>2nd</u> - Then let the corners of your mouth to turn up slightly. It is not necessary for others to see it, just for you to feel it.

<u>3rd</u> - Take on a peaceful facial expression. Keep in mind that your face communicates to your brain that everything will be okay.

Accepting Reality
WITH YOUR BODY

WILLING HANDS

WILLING HANDS is a way of accepting reality with your body and letting go of any upset you might be holding on to. By using WILLING HANDS, you're actually allowing yourself to move forward without feeling overwhelmed by stressful events. It's a great way to take care of yourself physically and mentally.

HOW TO DO WILLING HANDS

1st - STANDING: Lower your shoulders, turn the palms outward, loosen hands and fingers.

2nd - SEATED: Place your hands with the palms up and fingers relaxed on your lap as if you are willing to listen.

3rd - LYING DOWN: Place arms by your side, unclench hands, and relax your fingers.

How to Accept Reality
WITH YOUR BODY

- -

When you find it tough to TURN YOUR MIND, you can try out the HALF-SMILE and WILLING HANDS techniques to physically ACCEPT REALITY. By practicing these skills when you're stressed and also when you're calm, you can help train your brain to handle distress more easily.

WHEN TO PRACTICE
HALF-SMILE & WILLING HANDS

- Before getting out of bed in the morning

- When you have negative or racing thoughts

- When your emotions run high or your feelings get hurt

- While listening to music or watching tv

- When you feel overwhelmed by the situation

- When you do not want to accept something

- During free moments throughout the day

- When you begin to feel out of control or shut down

ACCEPTING REALITY

- -

HOW DID YOU PRACTICE HALF-SMILING AND WILLING HANDS TODAY?

Practice HALF-SMILING and WILLING HANDS every day
when you are both relaxed and emotionally distressed.

☐ While listening to music

☐ During social anxious situations

☐ When feeling angry or annoyed

☐ During moments of relaxation

☐ When spending time with friends

☐ When first waking up

☐ After something frustrating happens

☐ While walking down the street

☐ When not wanting to accept things

☐ While not felling in control

☐ Before going to bed at night

☐ When feeling hurt or upset

☐ During a disagreement with someone

☐ After being disappointed or let down

☐ While thinking negatively

☐ Other:_____

ACCEPTING REALITY

- - - - - - - - - - - - - - - - - - -

HOW DID YOU PRACTICE HALF-SMILING AND WILLING HANDS TODAY?

What happened?

How did you accept reality?

How did it affect your mood or reaction to the situation?

CAN YOU ACCEPT IT?

1) THE SITUATION: _____

_____

_____

_____

_____

2) WHAT ARE YOU HAVING DIFFICULTY ACCEPTING: _____

_____

_____

_____

_____

3) WHAT IS YOUR LEVEL OF RESISTING REALITY:

Not Happening   Whatever   It's All Good

⟵—————————————————————⟶

1   2   3   4   5

4) HOW WILLING ARE YOU TO ACCEPT THE SITUATION:

Not Happening   Whatever   It's All Good

⟵—————————————————————⟶

1   2   3   4   5

5) WHAT RADICAL ACCEPTANCE SKILL CAN YOU USE:

☐ Pros and Cons ☐ Half-Smile ☐ Willingness

☐ Turning the Mind ☐ Willing Hands ☐ Radical Acceptance

6) HOW EFFECTIVE WAS THE SKILL IN ACCEPTING THE SITUATION:

Nope   A Little   Absolutely

⟵————————————————————⟶

1   2   3   4   5

7) HOW DID THE SKILL HELP OR NOT HELP IN TRYING TO RADICALLY ACCEPT THE SITUATION: _____

_____

_____

_____

_____

8) WHAT ELSE CAN YOU DO TO ACCEPT THE SITUATION: _____

_____

_____

_____

_____

_____

9) WHAT RADICAL ACCEPTANCE SKILL CAN YOU USE:

☐ Pros and Cons ☐ Half-Smile ☐ Willingness

☐ Turning the Mind ☐ Willing Hands ☐ Radical Acceptance

10) HOW EFFECTIVE WAS THE SKILL IN ACCEPTING THE SITUATION:

Nope   A Little   Absolutely

⟵————————————————————⟶

1   2   3   4   5

11) HOW DID THE SKILL HELP OR NOT HELP IN TRYING TO RADICALLY ACCEPT THE SITUATION: _____

_____

_____

_____

12) WHAT ELSE CAN YOU DO TO ACCEPT THE SITUATION: _____

_____

_____

_____

_____

ROADMAP TO ACCEPTING REALITY

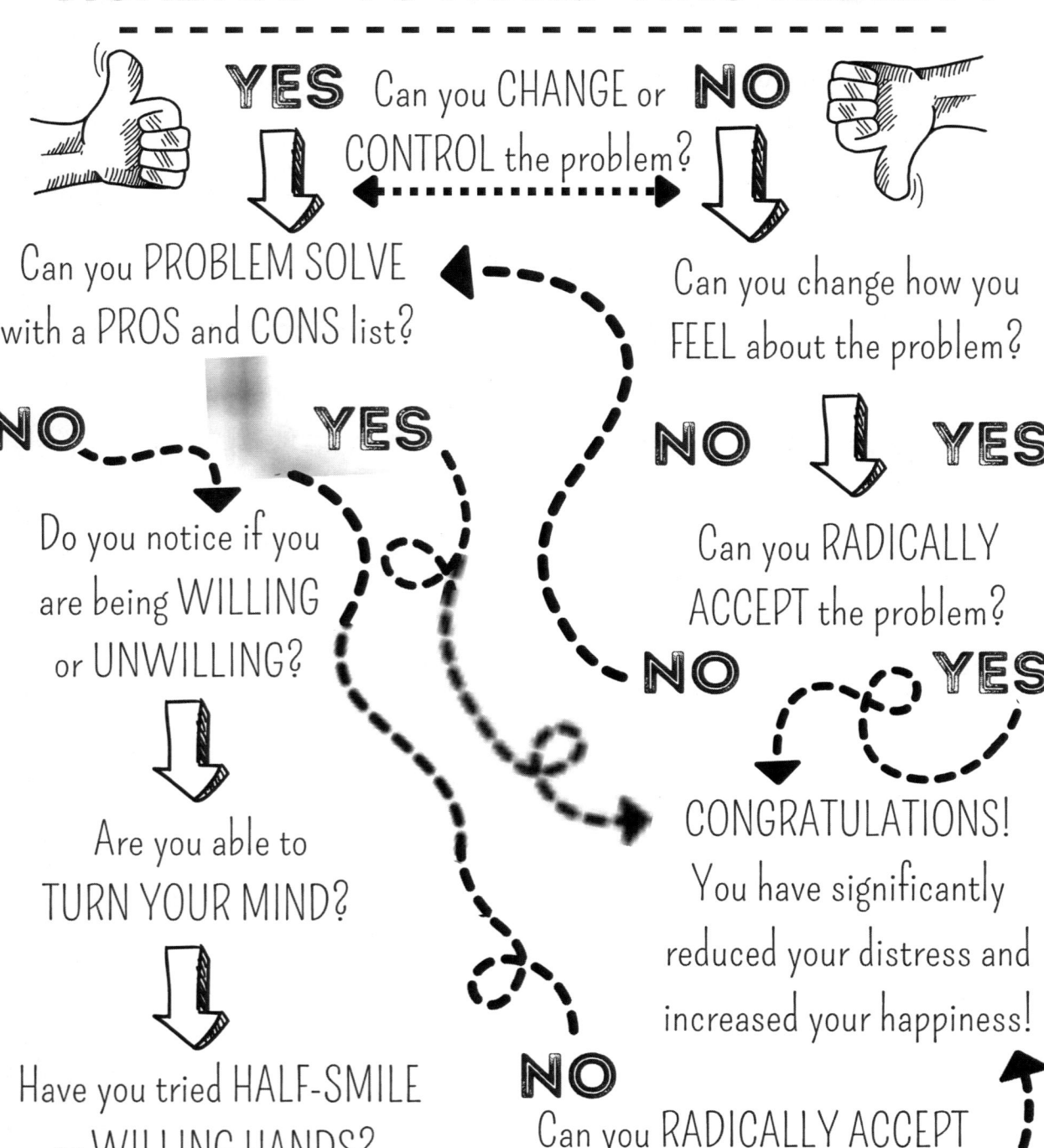

YES Can you CHANGE or CONTROL the problem? **NO**

Can you PROBLEM SOLVE with a PROS and CONS list?

Can you change how you FEEL about the problem?

NO **YES**

NO **YES**

Do you notice if you are being WILLING or UNWILLING?

Can you RADICALLY ACCEPT the problem?

NO **YES**

Are you able to TURN YOUR MIND?

CONGRATULATIONS! You have significantly reduced your distress and increased your happiness!

Have you tried HALF-SMILE or WILLING HANDS?

NO Can you RADICALLY ACCEPT the problem? **YES**

How do you
STAY TRUE TO YOURSELF?

FOCUSING ON WHAT REALLY MATTERS

DO-IT-YOURSELF-DBT
Radical Values And Strengths (PART 4)

RADICAL VALUES

Radical acceptance is all about fully and completely embracing what is happening in our lives, even if it's difficult or not what we expected. It's about recognizing that fighting against the reality of a situation only leads to suffering, and instead choosing to accept and adapt to what is. Now, personal values are those guiding principles that shape who we are and how we live our lives. They're like our compass, helping us make decisions that align with what truly matters to us. So when we combine radical acceptance with our personal values, it's like finding a harmonious balance between embracing what is and staying true to ourselves. It's about accepting the things we can't change and focusing on what really matters to us. It's a powerful mindset that can bring us peace and fulfillment!

WHAT'S UP WITH VALUES

Have you ever thought about how our values shape the way we see the world? They're like our own personal compass, guiding us towards what's important to us in life. And the best part? Everyone's values are totally unique to them! Things like friendship, family, and fun are just a few examples of values that people often cherish.

It's pretty cool to think about how our values influence the decisions we make. Whether it's choosing friends, deciding on a career path, or knowing what matters most to help us navigate life's twists and turns.

For instance, if you're all about adventure, you're probably someone who loves trying new things. A job that's too routine might not be your cup of tea, but if stability is more your style, a career in something like computer programming could be right up your alley.

Taking a closer look at our values can often shed some light on what's missing. It's important to align our daily actions with our values to lead a truly fulfilling life. So, don't forget to embrace what matters most to you and let it guide you towards happiness and meaning!

VALUES LIST

- Acceptance
- Activist
- Adventure
- Assertiveness
- Authenticity
- Comfort
- Commitment
- Community
- Confidence
- Connection
- Content
- Compassion
- Competition
- Courage
- Creativity
- Curiosity
- Democracy
- Diversity

- Empowerment
- Encouragement
- Equality
- Excitement
- Excellence
- Family
- Fairness
- Faith
- Fitness
- Flexibility
- Freedom
- Friendliness
- Forgiveness
- Fun
- Generosity
- Gratitude
- Happiness
- Honesty

- Humor
- Humility
- Independence
- Individuality
- Innovation
- Integrity
- Justice
- Kindness
- Leadership
- Love
- Loyalty
- Meaning
- Mindfulness
- Openminded
- Patience
- Peace
- Perfection
- Persistence

- Positive attitude
- Privacy
- Purpose
- Respect
- Responsibility
- Self-awareness
- Self-care
- Self-control
- Self-development
- Service
- Spirituality
- Success
- Supportiveness
- Tolerance
- Tradition
- Trust
- Wealth
- Wisdom

IDENTIFYING PERSONAL VALUES

Your values are like your own personal GPS guiding you through life. It's essential to take the time to define and adjust them so you can steer your life in the direction of your biggest dreams. Below are some questions to help you figure out what values truly matter to you!

- Who are the people you look up to most in your life and why?

- Who is your best friend, and what are their top three qualities?

- If you could have more of any one quality, what would it be?

- Which attribute or quality do people compliment you the most?

• What are some behaviors or attributes of people you dislike?

-- -- -- -- -- -- -- -- -- -- -- -- -- -- -- -- -- -- --
-- -- -- -- -- -- -- -- -- -- -- -- -- -- -- -- -- -- --
-- -- -- -- -- -- -- -- -- -- -- -- -- -- -- -- -- -- --

• What values do you need to achieve your future goals?

-- -- -- -- -- -- -- -- -- -- -- -- -- -- -- -- -- -- --
-- -- -- -- -- -- -- -- -- -- -- -- -- -- -- -- -- -- --
-- -- -- -- -- -- -- -- -- -- -- -- -- -- -- -- -- -- --

• What are you doing or experiencing when you are happy?

-- -- -- -- -- -- -- -- -- -- -- -- -- -- -- -- -- -- --
-- -- -- -- -- -- -- -- -- -- -- -- -- -- -- -- -- -- --
-- -- -- -- -- -- -- -- -- -- -- -- -- -- -- -- -- -- --

• What is something you have strong feelings about?

-- -- -- -- -- -- -- -- -- -- -- -- -- -- -- -- -- -- --
-- -- -- -- -- -- -- -- -- -- -- -- -- -- -- -- -- -- --
-- -- -- -- -- -- -- -- -- -- -- -- -- -- -- -- -- -- --

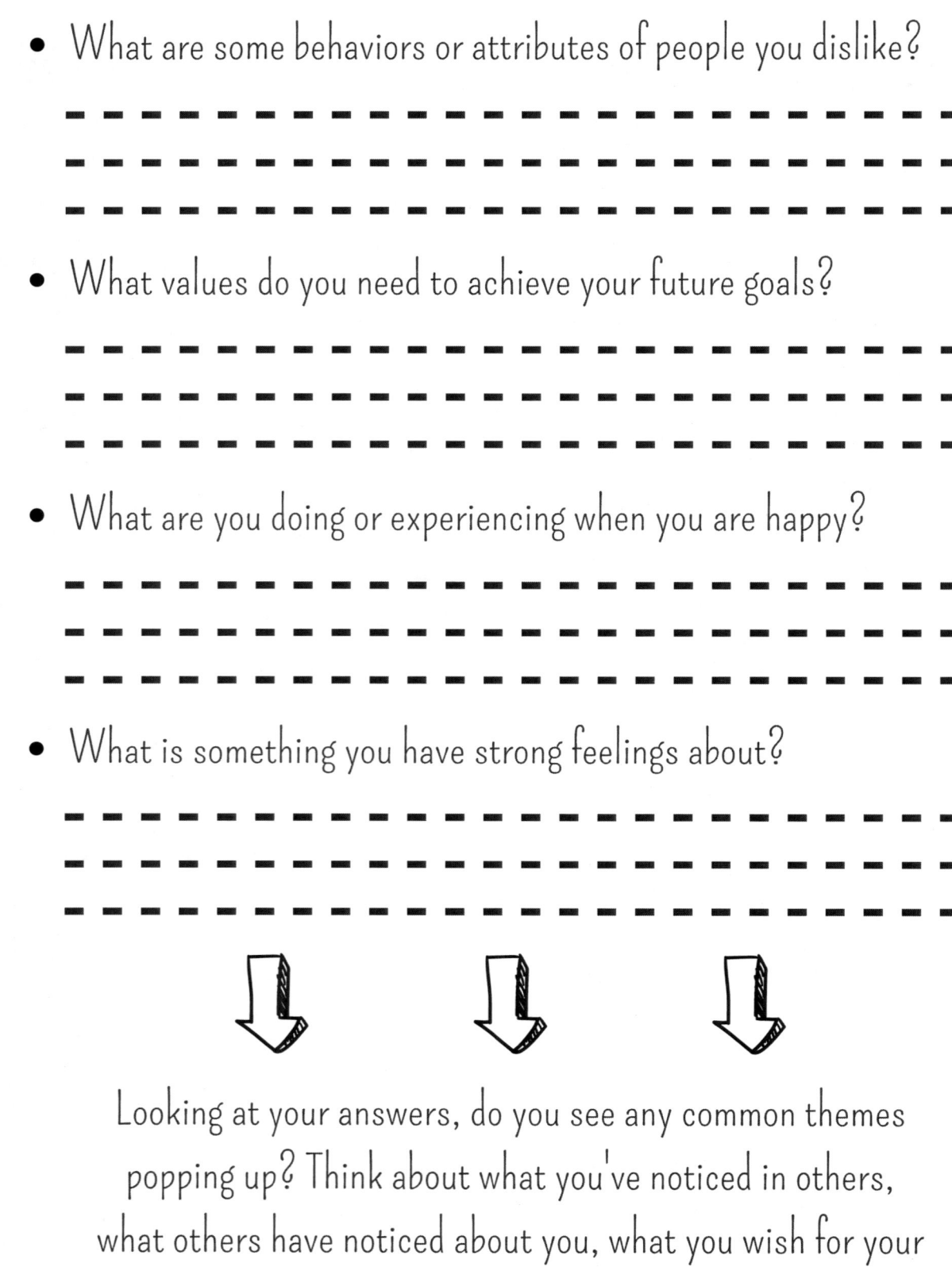

Looking at your answers, do you see any common themes popping up? Think about what you've noticed in others, what others have noticed about you, what you wish for your future, and the things you feel strongly about. Put together a list of your top 10 values based on these reflections.

WHAT ARE YOUR TOP 10 VALUES?

1) _____ 6) _____

2) _____ 7) _____

3) _____ 8) _____

4) _____ 9) _____

5) _____ 10) _____

Now, break that down to your top 5 values

WHAT ARE YOUR TOP 5 VALUES?

1) _____

2) _____

3) _____

4) _____

5) _____

Now, break that down to your top 3 values

WHAT ARE YOUR TOP 3 VALUES?

1) _____

2) _____

3) _____

HOW VALUES CAN CHANGE YOUR LIFE

Once you identify your personal values, then you can work them into all areas of your life and see how they influence your choices, give you purpose, and inspire your life experiences. Perhaps it's friendship, confidence, or happiness. If you had more of that value, how would it change your life? EXPLORE & HAVE FUN!!!

- What are some behaviors or attributes of people you dislike?

- What would be different in your friendships or relationships?

- What would change for you at home or in school?

- How would you treat yourself differently?

- How would you handle things differently in your life?

- How would you treat others differently?

- What kind of things would you start doing?

- What kind of things would you stop doing?

- What goals would you set for yourself?

- What actions would you take to improve your life?

LIVING YOUR VALUES

- VALUE: <u>Friendship</u>
  - ○ BEHAVIORS:
    - ■ <u>Expand social circle</u>
    - ■ <u>Resolve conflicts</u>
    - ■ <u>Be a good friend</u>
    - ■ <u>More quality time with friends</u>

- VALUE: _____
  - ○ BEHAVIORS:
    - ■ _____
    - ■ _____
    - ■ _____
    - ■ _____

- VALUE: _____
  - ○ BEHAVIORS:
    - ■ _____
    - ■ _____
    - ■ _____
    - ■ _____

- VALUE:_____
  - BEHAVIORS:
    - _____
    - _____
    - _____
    - _____

- VALUE:_____
  - BEHAVIORS:
    - _____
    - _____
    - _____
    - _____

- VALUE:_____
  - BEHAVIORS:
    - _____
    - _____
    - _____
    - _____

RELATIONSHIP VALUES

Many times, we find ourselves getting into relationships or friendships without really having a clear idea of what we want from them. But here's the thing: once we start understanding our own values better, it actually becomes much easier to form and maintain strong, healthy relationships.

When we have a good grasp of what truly matters to us, it becomes a guiding compass in our interactions with others. Understanding our values is like a superpower that empowers us to build stronger, more fulfilling relationships. So, let's utilize our values to create stronger connections!

- What qualities do you admire in a friend or partner?

....

....

- What are my favorite memories of time spent with your friend or partner?

....

....

- When does my friend or partner show me how much they care about and value me?

....

....

- Why do I value my friend or partner?

....

....

RELATIONSHIP VALUES:

- Trust
- Loyalty
- Spirituality
- Family/Friends
- Communication
- Lifestyle
- Interests

- Respect
- Self-improvement
- Conflict management
- Forgiveness
- Authenticity
- Empathy
- Independence

- Honesty
- Self-discipline
- Emotional support
- Kindness
- Personal Growth
- Adventure
- Humor

RADICAL STRENGTHS

Radical acceptance is all about wholeheartedly accepting ourselves, flaws and all. It's about acknowledging that we are imperfect beings, accepting our past mistakes, and embracing our present reality. But alongside radical acceptance, we also have an incredible arsenal of personal strengths. These strengths are our unique qualities, talents, and skills that make us who we are. They empower us to tackle challenges, develop resilience, and achieve personal growth. So, let's embrace radical acceptance and celebrate our personal strengths, because that's when we can truly shine and thrive in our own magnificent ways.

MY STRENGTHS

Active	Curious	Kind
Admirable	Easygoing	Lively
Adventurous	Educated	Loving
Agreeable	Enthusiastic	Loyal
Appreciative	Ethical	Nice
Athletic	Extraordinary	Optimistic
Authentic	Fair	Organized
Brave	Focused	Passionate
Brilliant	Forgiving	Peaceful
Calm	Friendly	Playful
Capable	Generous	Reliable
Caring	Gentle	Respectful
Charming	Grateful	Responsible
Cheerful	Happy	Self-disciplined
Clever	Hardworking	Strong
Compassionate	Helpful	Sweet
Confident	Honest	Thoughtful
Considerate	Hopeful	Trustworthy
Cooperative	Humble	Understanding
Courageous	Intelligent	Unselfish
Creative	Joyful	Wise

STRENGTHS SELF-ASSESSMENT

1. What do you like to do for fun?

2. What are you really good at?

3. Where do you like to spend time, and why do you like it there?

4. Who do you like to spend time with? Why do you like to spend time with them?

5. What is really important to you?

6. What would you like to have that you don't have right now?

7. Who would you really like to meet in person? What do you admire about this person?

8. If you had one wish to change something about your life, what would you wish for?

9. What is your favorite subject in school? Why do you like this subject?

10. Who is your favorite teacher? Why do you like him/her?

11. Who is your best friend at school? Why do you both get along so well?

12. What kinds of things make you angry? What do you do when you get angry?

13. What do you like about going to school? What don't you like about going to school?

14. When you "day dream" what do you think about?

15. What would you like to have as a job when you grow up?

16. What do you like best about yourself? What would you like to change about yourself?

17. What kinds of things do you do to take care of yourself?

18. Do you like sports? What is your favorite sport? Do you like to play this sport or watch?

19. When do you feel at your best?

20. If you had one wish to make something happen in your life, what would you wish for?

_____

What patterns jump out at you? Are there any common themes? What strengths stand out to you?

WHAT ARE YOUR STRENGTHS?

Take a moment to reflect on who you are as a person. Indicate whether each STRENGTH is mostly like you, sometimes like you, or not often like you. It's important to remember that everyone has their own unique strengths. You also have the power to develop new strengths anytime!

STRENGTH	DESCRIPTION	MOSTLY LIKE ME	SOMETIMES LIKE ME	NOT OFTEN LIKE ME
Judgment	I I love examining all perspectives of a problem to find the best solution.			
Fairness	I believe in treating everyone with fairness and justice.			
Teamwork	I I'm always happy to contribute and I put in a lot of effort to help my group succeed.d actions.			
Love of learning	I absolutely adore learning new things.			
Perseverance	I I always make sure to complete whatever I start, no matter how challenging it gets.			
Social intelligence	I always make sure to take note of how others are feeling and what's motivating them.			
Zest	I absolutely love living life as an adventure, always filled with excitement and energy.			

STRENGTH	DESCRIPTION	MOSTLY LIKE ME	SOMETIMES LIKE ME	NOT OFTEN LIKE ME
Bravery	I always make sure to stand up for what is right, even if others may not see eye to eye with me.			
Kindness	I really love helping others, even if I don't know them very well.			
Honesty	I always speak my mind and I'm accountable for my emotions and actions.			
Wisdom	I'm often seen as wise because I make a point to consider things from different perspectives.			
Creativity	I love brainstorming and coming up with new ideas to improve how things are done.			
Leadership	I'm really skilled at providing leadership and direction when I'm with a group of people.			
Love	I really value the special connections I have with others.			
Curiosity	I'm always curious and love exploring new things.			

YOUR EMOTIONAL STRENGTHS

Sometimes we tend to focus too much on our problems and forget about our emotional strengths we already possess to tackle these issues. Take a look at the list of statements below that highlight important emotional strengths. Simply rate each statement from 1 to 7, with 1 meaning "Strongly Disagree" and 7 meaning "Strongly Agree."

_____ I am so grateful for my ability to love others.

_____ I usually have a high level of self-esteem.

_____ Being a flexible person is one of my strengths.

_____ I love using my creativity in various aspects of my life.

_____ Curiosity drives me to explore and learn new things.

_____ Other people's don't hold me back from doing what I believe is right.

_____ I am assertive in looking out for the interests of those I care about.

_____ Setting realistic goals for myself helps me stay motivated a

_____ My good common sense guides me in making wise decisions.

_____ I have the ability to control my impulses.

_____ Taking care of my body and health is a priority for me.

_____ Being flexible allows me to adapt to different situations.

_____ I usually trust others and give them the benefit of the doubt.

_____ Even in stressful situations, I manage to stay calm.

_____ Patience is one of my virtues.

_____ I believe in the power of positive thinking.

_____ I take full responsibility for my choices and actions.

_____ I enjoy being around others, but I also appreciate my alone time.

_____ I have a knack for predicting how others will behave.

_____ I enjoy learning more about myself.

_____ When something is bothering me, I can usually identify it.

_____ My sense of humor is a great coping mechanism for stress.

_____ If I can't control a situation, I know how to stop worrying about it.

_____ I am grateful to have several close confidants in my life.

_____ When I need help, I have a reliable support network I can turn to.

_____ Expressing anger when necessary is not a problem for me.

_____ I have effective techniques to calm myself down when I'm upset.

_____ I accept and acknowledge my feelings, even when their difficult.

_____ Open and honest communication is important to me.

_____ When I make a mistake, I see it as an opportunity to learn and grow.

_____ I don't see myself as a victim; I take charge of my life.

_____ Uncertainty and the unknown don't bother me; I embrace them.

_____ Most of the time, I am easygoing and go with the flow.

STRENGTHS TO BOOST HAPPINESS

Did you know that you can use your unique character strengths to boost your happiness and make a positive impact on those around you? By recognizing and utilizing your strengths, you can not only benefit yourself but also spread joy to others. By tapping into your strengths and utilizing them in your daily life, you can boost your own happiness as well as spread positivity to others. So, let's explore together how you can make the most of your unique qualities to bring more joy and fulfillment into your life!

3 STEPS TO STRENGTHENING YOUR HAPPINESS

1. Pick one of your strengths that is at the core of who you are and gives you energy
2. Discover new way to express the strength every day
3. Express that strength a different way each day for at least 1 week

PUTTING IT INTO PRACTICE

Have you ever noticed how we often use our strengths without even realizing it? It's like second nature to us! But sometimes, it can be tough to think of new ways to utilize our strengths because we're so used to doing things a certain way. Let's challenge ourselves to get creative and explore different ways to make the most of our strengths. Who knows what amazing things we might discover!

So, when it comes to identifying your strengths, it can be super fun to think of practical examples. Let's say you want to explore how <u>ADVENTURE</u> can be used differently. Remember, you can keep it simple or make it as creative as you want - the choice is all yours!

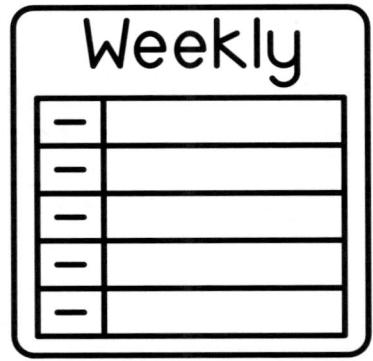

WEEKLY ADVENTURE EXAMPLES:

- On Monday, take the scenic route home from school or work to explore new surroundings as you drive.
- On Tuesday, ask one of your friends to go with you to try the new ice cream store that open up.
- On Wednesday, try a new food for lunch – something that seems interesting and part of your usual diet.
- On Thursday, go on a nature walk and see how many different animal species you encounter. Take photos!
- On Friday, introduce yourself to someone new at school who you have never really spoken with before. You might find a new friend!
- On Saturday, make a vision board with photos of all the places you would like to visit in your lifetime.
- On Sunday, take yourself on a field trip like to the zoo, a museum, a bookstore, the movies, etc...
- Next Monday....keep going!

RADICAL STRENGTHS FOR DAILY LIFE

- Curiosity - actively recognizing and pursuing challenging opportunities and seeking out new knowledge.
  - Find a person who shares your area of your interest and learn how he/she increases his/her expertise in that area.
  - Eat food of a different culture that you have little or no exposure to. Explore the food☒'s cultural context and become aware of your thoughts on it. Share a meal with a friend and compare your impressions.

- Creativity - applying your imaginations in new and surprising ways in order to solve the problems or focus on artistic expression.
  - Work on an article, essay, short story, poem, drawing, or painting in relation to your passion once a week. When you finish, look for a way to share your work with others who share your interest.
  - Redesign your room or home. Rearrange furniture to open up more floor space, even if you don't buy anything new.

- Open-mindedness - a willingness to consider evidence against one's own beliefs, plans, and goals, and to revise them if necessary.
    - Identify possible causes of past failures or disappointments. Are there any patterns? Take some time to think about how can you improve.
    - Identify the last three actions that you weren't happy with (such as not following through with a goal) and brainstorm better alternative ideas for the future. Consider both actions and omissions.

- Love of learning - enthusiastically studying new skills, topics, and bodies of knowledge.
    - Deliberately learn five new words, including their meaning and usage, at least twice a week. Use a dictionary, website, or word-a-day email list to generate new words.
    - Read a non-fiction book monthly on a topic you find absorbing and engaging. Find others who share your interest.

- Perspective - Being aware of thinking patterns, your own strengths and weaknesses, and the necessity of contributing to society.
    - Exercise optimism and patience with tasks that challenge you most. Remember how these tasks fit into the larger scheme of things.
    - Find purpose in the last five of your significant actions/decisions. Recall what motivated you to make the decisions that you made.

- Bravery - taking action without shrinking from the threats, challenges, or pain associated with attempting to do good works.
  - Resist social or peer pressure, instead choosing to act on noble values and causes in meaningful ways. For example, you can write, speak out, participate in a protest, or join an activist organization.
  - Don't be afraid to befriend someone who is different. Think of ways that their strengths as a friend can compliment your own.

- Persistence - Having the mental strength necessary to continue striving for one's goals in the face of obstacles and setbacks.
  - Plan a big project and finish it ahead of time. Don't be deterred by unexpected obstacles along the way.
  - Write your goals and aims and post them where they can inspire you regularly. Keep your list short enough that it doesn't seem overwhelming

- Integrity - Being open and honest about his or her own thoughts, feelings, and responsibilities, being careful not to mislead through either action or omission.
  - Monitor every time you tell a lie, even if it is a small one. Try to make your list shorter every day.
  - Think and act fairly when you face your next challenge, regardless of its impact on your position or popularity. Put aside your perceptions of peer pressure when making your decision.

- Vitality - approaching life marked with an appreciation for energy, liveliness, excitement, and energy.
  - Do a physical activity of your choice, one that you don't "have to do" and that you are not told to do. Notice how this affects your energy level.
  - Call an old friend and reminisce about good old times. Notice how their laughter and joy make you feel.

- Love - valuing close relationships with others, in particular those in which sharing and caring are reciprocated.
  - Explore and appreciate the strengths of your loved ones. Verbalize at least some of what you think in this area.
  - Express your love through gifts. When possible, create gifts yourself rather than buying them.

- Kindness - doing favors and good deeds for others without the expectation of personal gain.
  - Do three random acts of kindness per week for those whom you know. Consider doing small favors for friends and neighbors.
  - Say kinder and softer words to people when interacting through email, writing letters, talking on phone. Be aware that communication over distance requires different types of gentleness than face-to-face communication.

- Social Intelligence - Being aware of the emotions and intentions of yourself and others no matter what the social situation is; and attempting to make everyone involved feel comfortable and valued.
  - Listen to your friends and siblings empathically, without preparing rebuttals, and simply reflect your feelings after they are finished. Don't just wait for your turn to speak during conversation.
  - If someone offends you, attempt to find at least one positive element in his or her motives. Consider reasons why their offensive behavior.

- Citizenship - working as a member of a group for the common good and manifested through a sense of social belonging and civic responsibility.
  - Volunteer weekly for a community service project in your town, one that deals with what you are best at.
  - Volunteer for activities such as serving as a Big Brother or Big Sister or constructing a Habitat for Humanity house. Encourage friends and neighbors with spare time on their hands to accompany you.

- Fairness, Equity and Justice - True fairness incorporates both a respect for moral guidelines and a compassionate approach to caring for others.
  - The next time you make a mistake, self-monitor to see whether you admit it. Try to be more forthright about your mistakes in the future.
  - Watch a film or a documentary that exemplifies fairness, social justice, and equity. Think of how the topic relates to issues that you encounter in your own life.

- Leadership - the process of motivating, directing, and coordinating members of a group to achieve a common goal.
  - Listen to your friends and siblings empathically, without preparing rebuttals, and simply reflect your feelings after they are finished. Don't just wait for your turn to speak during conversation.
  - When two people are in an argument, mediate by inviting others to share their thoughts and emphasizing problem solving. Set a respectful, open-minded tone for the discussion.

- Forgiveness and Mercy - forgiving those who have wronged or offended us and accepting the shortcomings of others, giving people a second chance, and putting aside the temptation to hold a grudge or act out.
  - Make a list of individuals against whom you hold a grudge, then either meet them personally to discuss it and let bygones can be bygones.
  - Identify how a grudge tortures you emotionally. Does it produce disruptive emotions (anger, hatred, fear, worry, sadness, anxiety) Write three ways these disruptive emotions affect your behavior.

- Humility / Modesty - etting one's strengths and accomplishments speak for themselves
  - The next time you make a mistake, self-monitor to see whether you admit it. Try to be more forthright about your mistakes in the future.
  - Watch a documentary that exemplifies fairness and equity. Think of how the topic relates to issues that you encounter in your own life.

- Prudence - being careful about one's choices, not taking undue risks, and keeping long-term goals in mind when making short-term decisions.
  - Visualize the consequences of your decisions in one, five, and ten years time. Take these long-term consequences into account when making short-term choices.
  - Do a risk-benefit analysis before making a final decision. Consider risks and benefits that are intangible as well as tangible.

- Self-Regulation - exerting control over oneself in order to achieve goals or meet standards and control instinctive responses such as aggression and impulsivity.
  - Monitor and eliminate distractions such as phone, TV, and internet while focusing on a particular assignment. Allow yourself short breaks to avoid burnout.
  - Avoid talking about others in their absence. Don't solicit gossip from friends or co-workers.

- Appreciation of Beauty and Excellence -feeling a sense of awe at the world around them. They take pleasure in observing physical beauty, the skills and talents of other people,
  - Notice at least one instance of natural beauty around you every day (sunrise, sunset, clouds, sunshine, snowfall, rainbows, trees, moving leaves, birds chirping, flowers, fruits and vegetables, etc). Bring back the mental picture when your surroundings feel unpleasant.
  - Take pictures of natural scenes and share with friends.

- Gratitude - an awareness of and thankfulness for the good things and. expressing thanks for all you have been given in life.
  - Count three of your blessings (good things that happened to you) before going to bed every day. Write them down in a bedside journal for when you feel down or blue.
  - Express thanks to all who contributed to your success, no matter how small their contribution might have been.

- Hope - expecting good things will happen in the future including the best from themselves and others.
  - Recall a situation when you or someone close to you overcame a difficult obstacle and succeeded. Remember this precedent when you are faced with a similar situation
  - For the next three challenging tasks, identify what would work best for you: thinking your way into right action or acting your way into right thinking. Influence your future in a way that plays to your strengths.

- Humor -finding things to be cheerful about rather than letting adversity get you down; and enjoyment of laughing
  - Cheer up a gloomy friend. Be an example of how to approach life with a good-natured attitude.
  - Go out with your friends at least once a month for bowling, hiking, cross-country skiing, biking, and such. Note how the group dynamic improves when you laugh together.

- Spirituality - a universal part of the human experience involving knowledge of one's place within the larger scheme of things and awareness of the sacred in everyday life, . It can also include religious belief and practice.
    - Spend some time every day in at least one activity that connects you with a higher power or reminds you where you fit in the large scheme of things. Be mindful of your place in the larger context of life.
    - Spend ten minutes daily in breathing deeply, relaxing, or meditating (emptying the mind of thoughts by focusing on breathing).

STRENGTH IN RESILIENCE

STRENGTH     HOW IT SHOWS UP

Emotional Control: Manage your emotions so you can stay focused during tough times. People with this trait are also great at staying true to themselves no matter what situation they're in.	
Strong Relationships: Resilient people are great at staying connected with others and they often have really supportive relationships. They're also not afraid to ask for help or guidance from the people they trust.	
Authenticity and Self Acceptance: Living a life where our actions align with our beliefs and aspirations. It's all about walking the talk. Self-acceptance is about setting achievable goals, recognizing our strengths, and being aware of our weaknesses.	

Self Efficacy: Self efficacy is all about believing in yourself and your ability to achieve your goals. It's about staying focused and taking the necessary steps to make your dreams a reality.

Goal Setting: Setting goals is all about creating achievable targets and making steady progress towards them. Instead of getting overwhelmed by big, unrealistic goals, it's important to approach them with a clear and practical mindset.

Perspective: Resilient people have a great skill of keeping things in perspective when faced with tough times. Instead of immediately jumping to negative conclusions, they take a step back, stay calm, and assess the situation in a thoughtful way.

Curiosity: Being excited to learn new things! When it comes to being resilient, these qualities show that you're open to trying out different ways to overcome challenges and bounce back from tough situations.

Persistence: Persistence is such a key trait when it comes to resilience! It's all about pushing through those tough times and not giving up. But remember, it's also important to stay open to different ways of handling stress and tough situations.

Humor: A sense of humor enables you to not take yourself or your ideas too seriously. In doing so, you are better able to step back and observe circumstances with a little more detachment and objectivity.

I HAVE OVERCOME...

- What happened...

- How it affected me...

- What was the story I told myself about what happened...

- Some of the obstacles I faced...

- How I overcame it...

- What strengths did I use...

- Where did I find support...

- How did the story I tell myself about the experience change...

FLIP BOOK

Radical Acceptance
EMBRACING REALITY

LETTING GO OF WHAT YOU CANNOT CONTROL

DO-IT-YOURSELF-DBT
Reality Acceptance Skills (PART 1)

Do you ever get STUCK IN NEGATIVITY?

MOVING FORWARD WITH POSITIVITY

DO-IT-YOURSELF-DBT
Reality Acceptance Skills (PART 1)

WHY RADICALLY ACCEPT?

Not accepting the reality of a situation is linked to higher rates of emotional distress.

Practicing radical acceptance has been shown to reduce feelings of shame, guilt, sadness, and anxiety.

Radical acceptance increases happiness, improves relationships, and frees us from frustration.

RADICAL ACCEPTANCE CHEAT SHEET

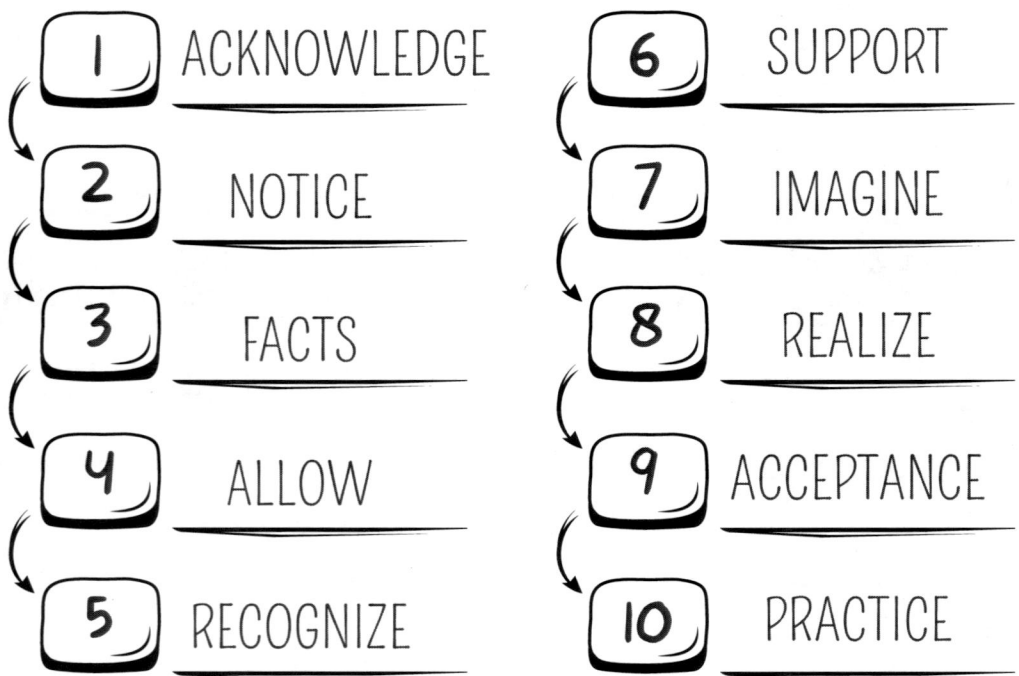

1	ACKNOWLEDGE	6	SUPPORT
2	NOTICE	7	IMAGINE
3	FACTS	8	REALIZE
4	ALLOW	9	ACCEPTANCE
5	RECOGNIZE	10	PRACTICE

FACTORS THAT INTERFERE WITH ACCEPTANCE

1. You believe that it is too difficult or you are incapable of accepting really painful events and facts.

2. You think by accepting an unwanted situation, you are "giving up" or will be unable to change or prevent any future upsets.

3. Your emotions such as anger, sadness, or shame get in the way of being able to accept the situation.

Radical Acceptance
COPING AFFIRMATIONS

- -

- I can handle what is in front of me as it is.
- Life is worth living, even if I am in pain.
- Life has ups and downs. Downs are inevitable.
- Fighting the past only blinds me from the present.
- I can live in the present, despite the pain I am experiencing.
- I can have pain without it turning into suffering.
- I can handle it, even if I am unhappy with what is happening.
- I can't change what has already happened.
- I can learn from the past to solve my present problems.
- My past does not define my future.
- How I react in this moment is all I have control over.
- I see the present moment for what it is.
- I can't change the situation, but I can control how I respond to it.
- I don't understand why this is happening, but I can accept it.
- This is how it has to be. I can't change the past.

How do you accept THINGS AS THEY ARE?

BEING OK WITH THINGS YOU CAN'T CHANGE

DO-IT-YOURSELF-DBT
Reality Acceptance Skills (PART 2)

Radical Acceptance
FOR CHANGE

---

① RADICAL ACCEPTANCE is about accepting the things you can't change.

② RADICAL ACCEPTANCE can reduce distress and increase feelings of freedom.

③ RADICAL ACCEPTANCE is when we are able to accept life just as it is, even if we don't like it.

WHEN IS ACCEPTANCE NEEDED?

- When stressful events happen in your life and you cannot fix them, change them, or make them go away.
- When you are you stuck in unhappiness, anger, shame, sadness, or other painful emotions from refusing to accept reality.
- When it's hard to accept things you don't like or that cause distress.
- When you want to work through difficulty but find it challenging.

ACCEPTANCE AND CHANGE

- -

I radically accept _____

And I will work to:

☐ Explore   ☐ Discover   ☐ Add

☐ Identify   ☐ Find   ☐ Change

☐ Move   ☐ Reduce   ☐ Not

☐ Help   ☐ Make   ☐ Think

☐ Apply   ☐ Close   ☐ Ask

       ☐ Follow-up   ☐ Switch

_____

_____

- -

I radically accept _____

And I will work to:

☐ Explore   ☐ Discover   ☐ Add

☐ Identify   ☐ Find   ☐ Change

☐ Move   ☐ Reduce   ☐ Not

☐ Help   ☐ Make   ☐ Think

☐ Apply   ☐ Close   ☐ Ask

       ☐ Follow-up   ☐ Switch

_____

_____

Accepting In The Moment
WHAT YOU CAN & CAN'T CONTROL

Do you ever find yourself wanting to have control over everything in your life? It's completely understandable, but it can be challenging to accept that we can't control everything. Although we may not have control over the world around us, we do have the ability to control our reactions to it.

By learning to accept and deal with situations that are out of our control, we can find inner peace and tranquility. This can also be beneficial in reducing stress and anxiety.

How do you
AVOID DISCOMFORT?

BREAKING THE CYCLE
OF ANXIETY & STRESS

DO-IT-YOURSELF-DBT
Reality Acceptance Skills (PART 3)

Common ways people
RESPOND TO DISCOMFORT

---

1) <u>Problem Solving</u> – Acknowledging the reality of the situation. Then changing what you can, and accepting what you cannot control.

2) <u>Changing The Outlook</u> - Finding meaning or value in the situation. Then looking at it from a more positive perspective to build acceptance.

3) <u>Turning the Mind</u> – Learning to tolerate the reality of the situation, even if you don't agree with it, and responding in a more confident way.

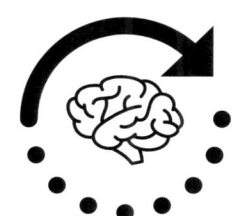

4) <u>Staying Miserable</u> – Resisting the reality of the situation, which will only worsen an already distressful and unhappy experience.

TURNING THE MIND

REJECTION 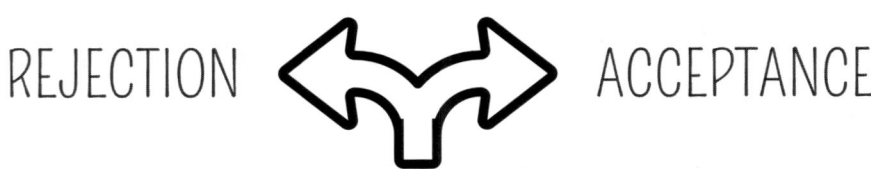 ACCEPTANCE

When presented with a situation we can't control, we can either choose REJECTION or ACCEPTANCE. Rejecting reality by trying to escape what is, blocking things out, or hiding emotions; can cause us to feel more distressed and resentful. If we can TURN THE MIND toward ACCEPTANCE, it puts us in the direction of calmness and joy.

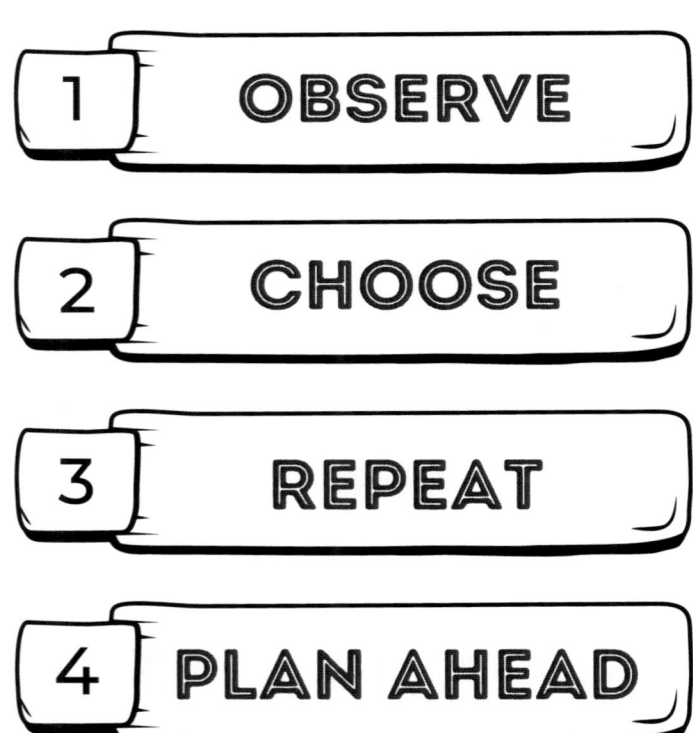

1 OBSERVE

2 CHOOSE

3 REPEAT

4 PLAN AHEAD

ROADMAP TO ACCEPTING REALITY

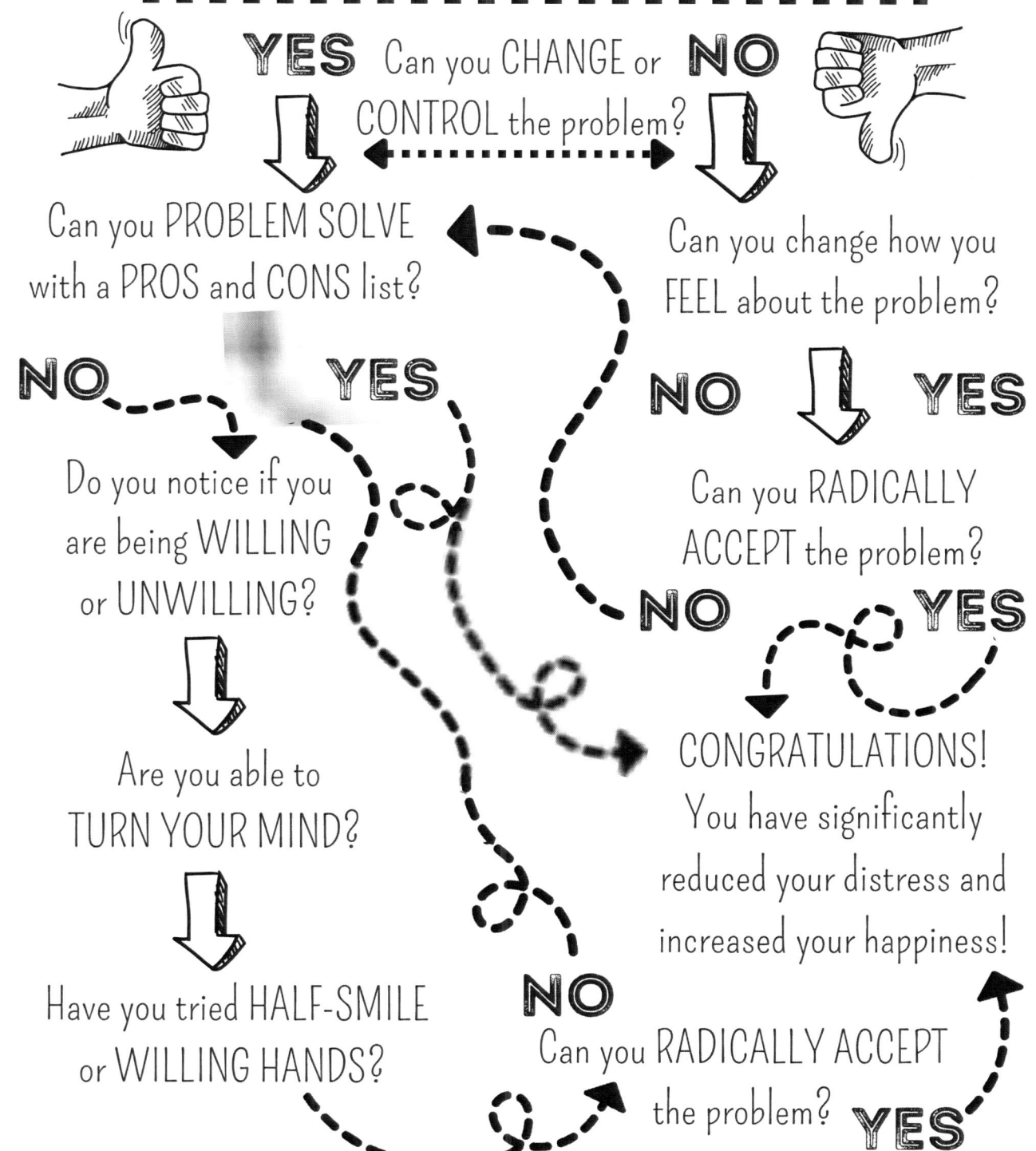

YES — Can you CHANGE or CONTROL the problem? — NO

Can you PROBLEM SOLVE with a PROS and CONS list?

Can you change how you FEEL about the problem?

NO   YES

NO   YES

Do you notice if you are being WILLING or UNWILLING?

Can you RADICALLY ACCEPT the problem?

NO   YES

Are you able to TURN YOUR MIND?

CONGRATULATIONS! You have significantly reduced your distress and increased your happiness!

Have you tried HALF-SMILE or WILLING HANDS?

NO — Can you RADICALLY ACCEPT the problem? — YES

Do-It-Yourself DBT

MINDFULNESS

DISTRESS
TOLERANCE

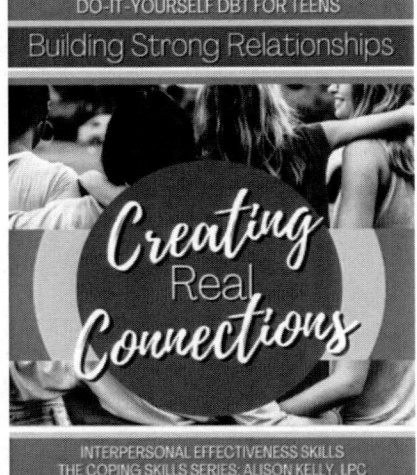

INTERPERSONAL
EFFECTIVENESS

RADICAL
ACCEPTANCE

EMOTION
REGULATION (PART 1)

EMOTION
REGULATION (PART 2)

www.CopingSkillsForTeens.com

Visit Our Websites

To Discover Books, Online Courses, Journals & Workbooks!

WWW.DOITYOURSELFDBT.COM

WWW.COPINGSKILLSFORTEENS.COM

Subscribe To Our Newsletter

Stay updated with NEW products, FREEBIES, and SPECIALS!

Connect With Us

DOITYOURSELFDBT@GMAIL.COM

MENTAL HEALTH DISCLAIMER

Check Out More Resources

THE COPING SKILLS FOR TEENS SERIES

Smash Your Social Anxiety

Anxiety Mind Traps

DO YOU EVER AVOID CERTAIN SOCIAL SITUATIONS?
BY ALISON KELLY, LPC - TEEN COUNSELOR

THE COPING SKILLS FOR TEENS SERIES

Body Posivity

Love The Skin You Are In

DO YOU STRUGGLE WITH YOUR BODY CONFIDENCE?
BY ALISON KELLY, LPC - TEEN COUNSELOR

THE COPING SKILLS FOR TEENS SERIES

Working Through Overthinking

A Plan For Procrastination

WHAT SITUATIONS, THINGS, OR PEOPLE DO YOU AVOID?
BY ALISON KELLY, LPC - TEEN COUNSELOR

THE COPING SKILLS FOR TEENS SERIES

Handling Stressful Situations

Coping With Confidence

HOW DO YOU COPE WITH TOUGH TIMES?
BY ALISON KELLY, LPC - TEEN COUNSELOR

THE COPING SKILLS FOR TEENS SERIES

Feel Good Thinking

Thinking Positive

HOW DO YOU CHALLENGE NEGATIVE THOUGHTS?
BY ALISON KELLY, LPC - TEEN COUNSELOR

THE COPING SKILLS FOR TEENS SERIES

Keeping Calm Under Stress

Stop Struggling With Stress

IS IT SOMETIMES DIFFICULT TO KEEP CALM?
BY ALISON KELLY, LPC - TEEN COUNSELOR

THE COPING SKILLS FOR TEENS SERIES

Overcoming Challenges

Skills For Resilience

DO YOU EVER FEEL OVERWHELMED OR OUT-OF-CONTROL?
BY ALISON KELLY, LPC - TEEN COUNSELOR

THE COPING SKILLS FOR TEENS SERIES

Put An End To Perfectionism

Unstick Your Thoughts

DOES YOUR PERFECTIONISTIC THINKING KEEP YOU STUCK?
BY ALISON KELLY, LPC - TEEN COUNSELOR

THE COPING SKILLS FOR TEENS SERIES

Boost Your Mood

Feel Good Feelings

HOW DO YOU SHOW YOURSELF AND OTHERS KINDNESS?
BY ALISON KELLY, LPC - TEEN COUNSELOR

www.CopingSkillsForTeens.com

RESOURCES

Linehan, M. M. (2014). DBT (R) skills training handouts and worksheets, second edition (2nd ed.). Guilford Publications.

Linehan, M., M., (2014). DBT Training Manual. New York, NY: The Guilford Press.

Mazza, J. J., & Dexter-Mazza, E. T. (2019). DBT skills in schools: Implementation of the DBT steps—A social emotional curriculum. In M. A. Swales (Ed.), The Oxford handbook of dialectical behaviour therapy (pp. 719–733). Oxford University Press.

Rathus, J. H., Miller, A. L., & Bonavitacola, L. (2019). DBT with adolescents. In M. A. Swales (Ed.), The Oxford handbook of dialectical behaviour therapy (pp. 547–572). Oxford University Press.

Made in United States
North Haven, CT
10 May 2024

52379031R00078